# • BAKE *and* MAKE •

# AMAZING

# COOKIES

Written by Elizabeth MacLeod
Illustrated by June Bradford

KIDS CAN PRESS

With lots of love to all my wonderful uncles:
Uncle Blair, Uncle Jack, Uncle Jim, and in memory of
Uncle Bud, Uncle Edgar, Uncle Gerry and Uncle John

Text © 2004 Elizabeth MacLeod
Illustrations © 2004 June Bradford

KIDS CAN DO IT and the 🦫 logo are trademarks of Kids Can Press Ltd.

Many of the designations used by manufacturers and sellers to distinguish their products are
claimed as trademarks. Where those designations appear in this book and Kids Can Press Ltd. was aware
of a trademark claim, the designations have been printed in initial capital letters (e.g., Life Savers).

Neither the Publisher nor the Author shall be liable for any damage that may be caused or sustained
as a result of conducting any of the activities in this book without specifically following instructions,
conducting the activities without proper supervision, or ignoring the cautions contained in the book.

Kids Can Press acknowledges the financial support of the Government of Ontario, through the
Ontario Media Development Corporation's Ontario Book Initiative, and the Government of Canada,
through the BPIDP, for our publishing activity.

Published in Canada by
Kids Can Press Ltd.
29 Birch Avenue
Toronto, ON  M4V 1E2

Published in the U.S. by
Kids Can Press Ltd.
2250 Military Road
Tonawanda, NY  14150

www.kidscanpress.com

Edited by Lori Burwash
Designed by Karen Powers

Printed in China by WKT Company Limited

The hardcover edition of this book is smyth sewn casebound.
The paperback edition of this book is limp sewn with a drawn-on cover.

CM 04  0 9 8 7 6 5 4 3 2 1
CM PA 04  0 9 8 7 6 5 4 3 2 1

National Library of Canada Cataloguing in Publication Data

MacLeod, Elizabeth
Bake and make amazing cookies / written by Elizabeth MacLeod; illustrated by June Bradford.

(Kids can do it)
ISBN 1-55337-631-5 (bound).      ISBN 1-55337-632-3 (pbk.)

1. Cookies — Juvenile literature. I. Bradford, June II. Title. III. Series.

TX772.M345 2004      j641.8'654      C2003-906476-X

Kids Can Press is a ℓ☉ℜ∪S™ Entertainment company

# Contents

# Introduction

*Mmmmmm! Is there anything better than homemade cookies? Cookies and squares are easy-to-make, delicious treats that make any day special. So why not celebrate Groundhog Day with Earthquakes? Or brighten a teacher's day with Crazy Daisies?*

*This book includes lots of ideas for celebrating holidays, people, seasons and "just for fun" days with cookies. There are even ideas for making your sweet treats extra special. And if you want to give cookies as presents, you'll find tips for wrapping them up. So what are you waiting for? Get baking!*

## MEASURING INGREDIENTS

Both the metric and imperial systems of measurement are used in this book. The systems are different, so choose one and use it for all your measuring.

Wet ingredients and dry ingredients require different measuring cups. A wet measuring cup has a spout to make pouring easier.

A dry measuring cup is flat across the top so you can use a knife to level off the ingredients.

If you're making cookies or squares for someone, make sure he or she isn't allergic to any of the ingredients, such as nuts or dairy products. Always carefully clean your utensils and work surface after making each recipe.

## CUTTING OUT DOUGH

Put a large piece of wax paper on a table or countertop. (A dab of water under each corner will hold the paper in place.) Sprinkle a little flour on the wax paper and on a rolling pin.

Place cookie dough on the wax paper and roll it out to the thickness or size suggested in the recipe. Cut out the cookies with cookie cutters dipped in flour. Use a lifter to transfer your cookies to a prepared baking sheet. Combine leftover dough, roll again and repeat until you've used up all the dough.

## BAKING

You'll find it faster and easier to make cookies if you use several baking sheets. It's also a good idea to use baking sheets and pans lined with aluminum foil.

Bake cookies, one sheet at a time, in the center of your oven. Cooking times vary from oven to oven, so bake for the minimum time suggested, then check.

Most cookies are baked when golden and firm to the touch. Squares are done when they're firm in the middle and have pulled away from the sides of the pan.

## STORING COOKIES

When your cookies are completely cool, place them in an airtight container with wax paper between the layers. Unless otherwise stated in the recipe, keep them at room temperature for up to 1 week or in the freezer for up to 2 months.

## MELTING CHOCOLATE AND BUTTER

Chocolate burns easily, so ask an adult to help you melt it in a microwave or double boiler. Heat chocolate slowly, just enough to melt it, stirring frequently.

If using a microwave, stir the chocolate at least every 30 seconds. If using a double boiler, place it on low heat. You can melt chips, squares or bars — cut up bars to help them melt faster.

Butter should be melted the same way as chocolate. Heat it slowly and get an adult to help you.

> Use thick oven mitts to handle hot saucepans or baking pans and sheets. Ask an adult to help move things into and out of the oven.

# New Year's icy shortbread

*Wish your friends Happy New Year with minty cookies.*

## YOU WILL NEED

| | | |
|---|---|---|
| 500 mL | butter (room temperature) | 2 c. |
| 250 mL | brown sugar (lightly packed) | 1 c. |
| | peppermint flavoring | |
| 1 L | all-purpose flour | 4 c. |
| 125 mL | crushed candy canes | ½ c. |

large mixing bowl, wooden spoon,
wax paper, rolling pin, cookie cutters, lifter,
baking sheet lined with aluminum foil,
cooling rack

1 Preheat the oven to 155°C (315°F).

2 Beat together the butter and sugar until creamy. Mix in 12 drops of peppermint flavoring. Add the flour and mix thoroughly.

3 Following the instructions on page 5, roll out some dough until it is 0.5 cm (¼ in.) thick. Cut out cookies using the cookie cutters. With the lifter, transfer cookies to the baking sheet, placing them about 2.5 cm (1 in.) apart. Repeat with remaining dough. Sprinkle a little crushed candy cane on each cookie.

4 Bake 12 to 15 minutes, until just firm and very pale. Cool for 5 minutes, then transfer cookies to the cooling rack. Cool completely.

*Makes about 5 dozen cookies*

## OTHER IDEAS

★ Instead of flavoring and candy, add 175 mL (¾ c.) chocolate chips, chopped pecans or walnuts, or dried cranberries.

# Groundhog Day earthquakes

*When the groundhog pokes its head out on February 2, celebrate with these cookies.*

## YOU WILL NEED

| | | |
|---|---|---|
| 250 mL | white sugar | 1 c. |
| 175 mL | butter (room temperature) | ¾ c. |
| 2 | eggs | 2 |
| 500 mL | all-purpose flour | 2 c. |
| 125 mL | unsweetened cocoa powder | ½ c. |
| 5 mL | baking powder | 1 tsp. |
| 5 mL | baking soda | 1 tsp. |
| 125 mL | icing sugar | ½ c. |

large mixing bowl, wooden spoon, sifter, small plate, baking sheet lined with aluminum foil, lifter, cooling rack

1 Preheat the oven to 180°C (350°F).

2 Beat together the white sugar and butter until creamy. Stir in the eggs. Sift the flour, cocoa, baking powder and baking soda into the butter mixture. Blend well.

3 Form the dough into 2.5 cm (1 in.) balls. Pour the icing sugar onto the plate, then roll the balls in the sugar. Place on the baking sheet about 4 cm (1½ in.) apart.

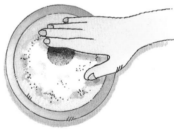

4 Bake 8 to 10 minutes, until the sugar has cracked. Cool for 5 minutes, then transfer cookies to the cooling rack. Cool completely.

*Makes about 5 dozen cookies*

## OTHER IDEAS

★ Make super chocolatey cookies by adding 250 mL (1 c.) chocolate chips.

# Sugar cookie valentines

*The sweetest way to say "I love you."*

## YOU WILL NEED

| | | |
|---|---|---|
| 250 mL | white sugar | 1 c. |
| 125 mL | shortening (room temperature) | ½ c. |
| 1 | egg | 1 |
| 5 mL | vanilla | 1 tsp. |
| 425 mL | all-purpose flour | 1¾ c. |
| 5 mL | baking powder | 1 tsp. |
| 1 mL | salt | ¼ tsp. |
| 500 mL | icing sugar | 2 c. |
| 50 mL | butter (room temperature) | ¼ c. |
| 45 mL | milk | 3 tbsp. |
| 2 mL | vanilla | ½ tsp. |
| | red food coloring | |
| | candies for decoration | |

large mixing bowl, wooden spoon, wax paper, rolling pin, heart-shaped cookie cutter, lifter, baking sheet lined with aluminum foil, cooling rack, medium mixing bowl

1 Preheat the oven to 180°C (350°F).

2 In the large bowl, beat together the sugar and shortening until creamy. Stir in the egg and 5 mL (1 tsp.) vanilla. Add the flour, baking powder and salt. Blend well.

3 Following the instructions on page 5, roll out some dough until it is 0.5 cm (¼ in.) thick. Cut out cookies using the cookie cutter. With the lifter, transfer cookies to the baking sheet, placing them about 4 cm (1½ in.) apart. Repeat with remaining dough.

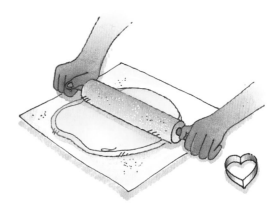

4 Bake 10 to 12 minutes, until golden. Cool for 2 minutes, then transfer cookies to the cooling rack. Cool completely.

5 For the icing, beat together the icing sugar, butter, milk and vanilla in the medium bowl until creamy. Stir in about 6 drops of food coloring to tint the icing pink. Spread icing on the cookies and decorate with candies.

*Makes about 2 dozen cookies*

## OTHER IDEAS

★ Tint half the dough pink using red food coloring. Roll out the plain dough and cut out cookies using a heart-shaped cookie cutter. Use a small heart-shaped cookie cutter to cut out the centers. Repeat with the pink dough, then put the pink centers in the plain outlines and the plain centers in the pink outlines.

★ Roll out the dough until it is 0.3 cm (⅛ in.) thick and cut out the cookies. Bake for about 8 minutes, until golden. When cool, sandwich two cookies together with strawberry jam.

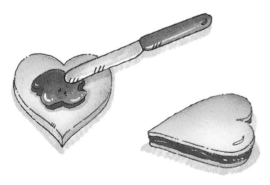

★ Make chocolate sugar cookies by replacing 50 mL (¼ c.) flour with 50 mL (¼ c.) sifted unsweetened cocoa powder.

## WRAP IT UP

★ Cut out a large paper heart and write a special message in the middle.

Wrap a cookie in wax paper or plastic wrap and place it on the message.

Fold the heart into a square around the cookie — folding the sides in first, then the top, then the bottom — and tape in place.

Carefully write the receiver's name on the other side and decorate the paper, if you like.

# St. Patrick's Day squares

*Better than a leprechaun's pot of gold!*

## YOU WILL NEED

| | | |
|---|---|---|
| 125 mL | butter | ½ c. |
| 50 mL | white sugar | ¼ c. |
| 1 | egg (beaten) | 1 |
| 75 mL | unsweetened cocoa powder | ⅓ c. |
| 500 mL | graham wafer crumbs | 2 c. |
| 250 mL | desiccated coconut | 1 c. |
| 125 mL | chopped walnuts | ½ c. |
| 50 mL | butter (room temperature) | ¼ c. |
| 500 mL | icing sugar | 2 c. |
| 15 mL | milk | 1 tbsp. |
| | green food coloring | |
| | peppermint flavoring | |
| 4 | squares semisweet chocolate | 4 |
| 15 mL | butter | 1 tbsp. |

medium saucepan, sifter, wooden spoon, 20 cm (8 in.) square cake pan lined with aluminum foil, medium mixing bowl, table knife, small mixing bowl

1 For the bottom layer, place 125 mL (½ c.) butter, the white sugar and egg in the saucepan. Sift the cocoa over the mixture. With an adult's help, stir over medium heat until the mixture thickens slightly, about 1 minute.

2 Remove from heat and stir in the graham crumbs, coconut and walnuts. Pat firmly into the pan. Refrigerate for at least 1 hour.

3 For the filling, cream 50 mL (¼ c.) butter in the medium bowl, then add the icing sugar, milk, 4 drops of food coloring and 8 drops of peppermint. Mix well.

4 Spread the filling over the bottom layer and refrigerate for about 30 minutes, until firm.

5 With an adult's help, melt the chocolate and butter (page 5), and mix together in the small bowl. Carefully spread the melted mixture over the filling. Refrigerate for about 5 minutes, then cut into squares.

Refrigerate for up to 2 weeks.

*Makes about 2 dozen squares*

# Easter egg nests

*You'll be more popular than the Easter bunny when you make jellybean nests.*

## YOU WILL NEED

| | | |
|---|---|---|
| 750 mL | chow mein noodles (broken in half) | 3 c. |
| 250 mL | sweetened flaked (or shredded) coconut | 1 c. |
| 50 mL | butter | ¼ c. |
| 750 mL | miniature marshmallows | 3 c. |
| 5 mL | vanilla | 1 tsp. |
| | butter | |
| 125 mL | small jellybeans | ½ c. |

large bowl, medium saucepan, wooden spoon, baking sheet lined with wax paper

**1** Place noodles and coconut in the bowl.

**2** With an adult's help, melt 50 mL (¼ c.) butter in the saucepan over medium heat, stirring constantly. Add marshmallows and stir until smooth. Remove from heat and stir in vanilla. Pour mixture over noodles and coconut, stirring until well coated.

**3** With a little butter on your fingers, drop small clumps of the noodle mixture onto the baking sheet. With your index finger or thumb, make an indent in the center of each clump. Quickly fill each indent with a few jellybeans.

Refrigerate for up to 2 weeks.

*Makes about 3 dozen nests*

## WRAP IT UP

★ Glue wide strips of felt or paper around a canister. Cover where the strips meet with ribbon or rickrack.

# Halloween howlers

*Purrfect Halloween treats!*

## YOU WILL NEED

| | | |
|---|---|---|
| 250 mL | brown sugar (lightly packed) | 1 c. |
| 75 mL | butter (room temperature) | ⅓ c. |
| 75 mL | shortening (room temperature) | ⅓ c. |
| 1 | egg | 1 |
| 45 mL | orange juice | 3 tbsp. |
| 10 mL | vanilla | 2 tsp. |
| 500 mL | all-purpose flour | 2 c. |
| 175 mL | unsweetened cocoa powder | ¾ c. |
| 5 mL | baking powder | 1 tsp. |
| 25 mL | white sugar | 2 tbsp. |
| 125 mL | chocolate M&M's | ½ c. |
| 25 mL | small red candies | 2 tbsp. |

large mixing bowl, wooden spoon, sifter, baking sheet lined with aluminum foil, small plate, flat-bottomed glass, fork, lifter, cooling rack

**1** Preheat the oven to 180°C (350°F).

**2** Beat together the brown sugar, butter and shortening until creamy. Stir in the egg, orange juice and vanilla. Sift in the flour, cocoa and baking powder. Blend well.

**3** Form the dough into 3 cm (1¼ in.) balls and place on the baking sheet about 4 cm (1½ in.) apart. Pour the white sugar onto the plate. Dip the glass bottom in the sugar, then flatten a ball with it. Repeat for each ball. Pinch ears, and add M&M's eyes and a red nose. Make whiskers by pressing the fork into the dough.

**4** Bake 10 to 12 minutes, until firm. Cool for 3 minutes, then transfer cookies to the cooling rack. Cool completely.

*Makes about 2½ dozen cookies*

## OTHER IDEAS

★ Don't decorate the faces before baking. When cookies are cool, spread with icing, then add candy eyes and nose, shoestring licorice whiskers and candy-corn ears.

# Thanksgiving hermits

*The recipe for these spicy cookies is almost as old as the first Thanksgiving.*

## YOU WILL NEED

| | | |
|---|---|---|
| 250 mL | brown sugar (lightly packed) | 1 c. |
| 125 mL | butter (room temperature) | ½ c. |
| 2 | eggs | 2 |
| 45 mL | orange juice | 3 tbsp. |
| 5 mL | vanilla | 1 tsp. |
| 500 mL | all-purpose flour | 2 c. |
| 5 mL | baking soda | 1 tsp. |
| 5 mL | ground cinnamon | 1 tsp. |
| 2 mL | ground allspice | ½ tsp. |
| 2 mL | ground nutmeg | ½ tsp. |
| 1 mL | salt | ¼ tsp. |
| 250 mL | raisins | 1 c. |
| 175 mL | chopped walnuts | ¾ c. |

large mixing bowl, wooden spoon, teaspoon, baking sheet lined with aluminum foil, lifter, cooling rack

**1** Preheat the oven to 180°C (350°F).

**2** Beat together the sugar and butter until creamy. Stir in the eggs, orange juice and vanilla. Add the flour, baking soda, spices and salt. Mix well. Stir in the raisins and walnuts.

**3** Drop the dough by teaspoonful onto the baking sheet about 4 cm (1½ in.) apart.

**4** Bake 10 to 12 minutes, until golden. Cool for 3 minutes, then transfer cookies to the cooling rack. Cool completely.

*Makes about 3½ dozen cookies*

## OTHER IDEAS

★ Replace the raisins and walnuts with 375 mL (1½ c.) chocolate chips or small gumdrops or 425 mL (1¾ c.) trail mix.

# Gingerbread reindeer

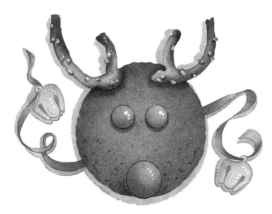

*What a great Christmas combination — gingerbread and reindeer.*

## YOU WILL NEED

| | | |
|---|---|---|
| 75 mL | shortening (room temperature) | 1/3 c. |
| 75 mL | brown sugar (lightly packed) | 1/3 c. |
| 1 | egg | 1 |
| 150 mL | molasses | 2/3 c. |
| 675 mL | all-purpose flour | 2¾ c. |
| 5 mL | baking powder | 1 tsp. |
| 5 mL | ground ginger | 1 tsp. |
| 2 mL | ground cinnamon | ½ tsp. |
| | mini pretzels (broken in half) | |
| | candies for decoration | |

large mixing bowl, wooden spoon, wax paper, rolling pin, round cookie cutter (or a glass or a jar lid), lifter, baking sheet lined with aluminum foil, cooling rack

1 Preheat the oven to 190°C (375°F).

2 Beat together the shortening and sugar until fluffy. Stir in the egg and molasses. Add the flour, baking powder, ginger and cinnamon. Blend well.

3 Following the instructions on page 5, roll out some dough until it is 0.5 cm (¼ in.) thick. Cut out cookies using the cookie cutter. With the lifter, transfer cookies to the baking sheet, placing them about 5 cm (2 in.) apart. Repeat with remaining dough. Add pretzel pieces for antlers and candies for eyes and a nose.

4 Bake 10 to 12 minutes, until firm. Cool for 3 minutes, then transfer cookies to the cooling rack. Cool completely.

*Makes about 3 dozen cookies*

## OTHER IDEAS

★ Create stained-glass cookies by rolling out some dough until it is 0.5 cm (¼ in.) thick. Cut out cookies using cookie cutters, then cut holes in each with a smaller cookie cutter or a knife. Transfer cookies to the baking sheet, then fill each hole with a different color of crushed Life Savers candy. With a straw, poke a hole near the edge of each cookie. Bake and cool cookies, then string ribbon through each hole and hang as decorations.

★ Make a jigsaw puzzle by rolling out dough until it is 0.5 cm (¼ in.) thick. Cut out a rectangle, any size you like. Bake for about 12 minutes — the time will depend on the size. As soon as you take the cookie out of the oven, ask an adult to help cut it into puzzle pieces. When the cookie is completely cool, ice and decorate it.

★ You can use this dough to make a gingerbread house, but make it a little stronger by kneading it first.

★ Make chocolate gingerbread by replacing 125 mL (½ c.) flour with sifted unsweetened cocoa powder and adding 250 mL (1 c.) chocolate chips.

## WRAP IT UP

★ Make a Christmas tree gift bag. Arrange lengths of ribbon across a cloth or paper bag so that the shortest is at the top and the longest at the bottom. Cut a piece of ribbon a little longer than the tree is tall. Glue it down the middle of the other ribbons. Dab glue at the tips of the ribbons, if you like.

# Butterscotch squares

*Your grandparents will love these treats on Grandparents Day (the first Sunday after Labor Day).*

## YOU WILL NEED

| | | |
|---|---|---|
| 1 | egg | 1 |
| 250 mL | brown sugar (lightly packed) | 1 c. |
| 50 mL | butter, melted (page 5) | ¼ c. |
| 10 mL | vanilla | 2 tsp. |
| 175 mL | all-purpose flour | ¾ c. |
| 5 mL | baking powder | 1 tsp. |
| 1 mL | salt | ¼ tsp. |
| 75 mL | chopped walnuts | ⅓ c. |
| 75 mL | sweetened flaked (or shredded) coconut | ⅓ c. |

large mixing bowl, wooden spoon, 20 cm (8 in.) square cake pan lined with aluminum foil, cooling rack

1 Preheat the oven to 180°C (350°F).

2 Beat together the egg, sugar, butter and vanilla until smooth. Blend in the flour, baking powder and salt. Stir in the walnuts and coconut.

3 Spread the mixture evenly in the pan. Bake 20 to 25 minutes, until light golden. Cool completely in the pan on the cooling rack.

*Makes about 2 dozen squares*

## OTHER IDEAS

★ Replace the coconut with chocolate chips or dried cranberries.

## WRAP IT UP

★ Cut out a felt shape, such as a heart or something special to your grandparent. Decorate it, then glue it to cardboard cut the same size and shape. Glue the cardboard to a clothespin and let dry. Use it to hold a bag of treats closed.

# Cookie pizza

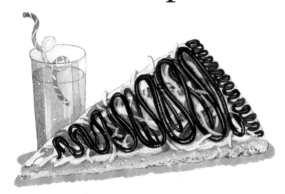

*A great birthday surprise for a friend.*

## YOU WILL NEED

| | | |
|---|---|---|
| 125 mL | butter (room temperature) | ½ c. |
| 125 mL | brown sugar (lightly packed) | ½ c. |
| 50 mL | white sugar | ¼ c. |
| 1 | egg | 1 |
| 300 mL | all-purpose flour | 1¼ c. |
| 2 mL | baking soda | ½ tsp. |
| 375 mL | icing sugar | 1½ c. |
| 50 mL | butter (room temperature) | ¼ c. |
| 25 mL | milk | 2 tbsp. |
| 2 mL | vanilla | ½ tsp. |
| 125 mL | pecan halves | ½ c. |
| | candies for decoration | |
| 50 mL | sweetened flaked (or shredded) coconut | ¼ c. |
| 50 mL | chocolate chips | ¼ c. |

large mixing bowl, wooden spoon,
large baking sheet lined with aluminum foil,
cooling rack, medium mixing bowl,
teaspoon

1 Preheat the oven to 180°C (350°F).

2 In the large bowl, beat together 125 mL (½ c.) butter and the sugars until creamy. Stir in the egg. Add the flour and baking soda. Blend well.

3 Pat the dough on the baking sheet into a circle about 30 cm (12 in.) across. Bake 15 minutes, until golden. Cool completely on the sheet on the cooling rack.

4 For the icing, beat together the icing sugar, butter, milk and vanilla in the medium bowl until creamy. Spread icing on the cookie, then sprinkle it with pecans, candies and coconut. With an adult's help, melt the chocolate chips (page 5), then drizzle on the chocolate.

Store the undecorated cookie at room temperature for up to 1 week or freeze for up to 2 months.

*Makes 12 to 16 slices*

## OTHER IDEAS

★ Make a pizza shaped like a football, star or dog — whatever your friend likes — and decorate it.

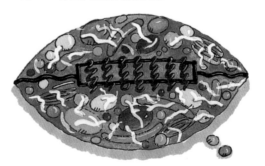

# Triple chocolate cookies

*What better cookie for a chocolate lover?*

## YOU WILL NEED

| | | |
|---|---|---|
| 250 mL | margarine (room temperature) | 1 c. |
| 175 mL | brown sugar (lightly packed) | ¾ c. |
| 125 mL | white sugar | ½ c. |
| 2 | eggs | 2 |
| 5 mL | vanilla | 1 tsp. |
| 400 mL | all-purpose flour | 1⅔ c. |
| 75 mL | unsweetened cocoa powder | ⅓ c. |
| 5 mL | baking soda | 1 tsp. |
| 2 mL | salt | ½ tsp. |
| 250 mL | white chocolate chips | 1 c. |
| 250 mL | chocolate chips | 1 c. |
| 250 mL | chopped pecans | 1 c. |

large mixing bowl, wooden spoon, sifter, teaspoon, baking sheet lined with aluminum foil, lifter, cooling rack

1 Preheat the oven to 190°C (375°F).

2 Beat together the margarine and sugars until creamy. Stir in the eggs and vanilla. Sift the flour, cocoa, baking soda and salt over the mixture. Mix well. Stir in the remaining ingredients.

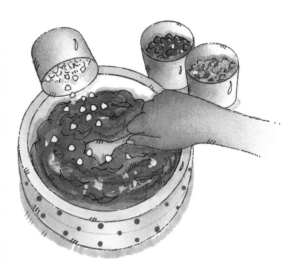

3 Drop the dough by teaspoonful onto the baking sheet about 5 cm (2 in.) apart.

4 Bake 8 to 10 minutes, until firm. Cool for 1 minute, then transfer cookies to the cooling rack. Cool completely.

*Makes about 4 dozen cookies*

## OTHER IDEAS

★ Replace the pecans with milk chocolate or butterscotch chips.

# Lucky seven squares

*Seven is a lucky number, so wish a friend good luck with seven-ingredient squares.*

## YOU WILL NEED

| | | |
|---|---|---|
| 125 mL | butter, melted (page 5) | ½ c. |
| 250 mL | graham wafer crumbs | 1 c. |
| 250 mL | sweetened flaked (or shredded) coconut | 1 c. |
| 250 mL | butterscotch chips | 1 c. |
| 250 mL | chocolate chips | 1 c. |
| 1 | 300 mL (10 oz.) can sweetened condensed milk | 1 |
| 250 mL | chopped pecans | 1 c. |
| | 23 cm x 33 cm (9 in. x 13 in.) cake pan lined with aluminum foil, fork, cooling rack | |

1 Preheat the oven to 180°C (350°F).

2 Pour the melted butter into the pan. Sprinkle the graham crumbs over the butter and press firmly with the fork.

3 Sprinkle on the coconut, then the butterscotch chips, then the chocolate chips. Pour the condensed milk evenly over top. Sprinkle on the pecans and press firmly with the fork.

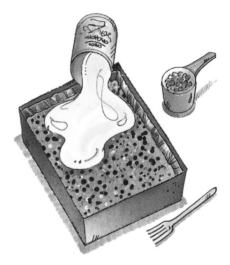

4 Bake 30 minutes, until edges are lightly browned. Cool completely in the pan on the cooling rack.

*Makes about 6 dozen squares*

## OTHER IDEAS

★ Replace the graham wafer crumbs with chocolate wafer crumbs.

★ Replace butterscotch chips with candied fruit or white chocolate chips.

# Oatmeal dinos

*Dino-mite cookies for dinosaur fans.*

## YOU WILL NEED

| | | |
|---|---|---|
| 250 mL | shortening (room temperature) | 1 c. |
| 250 mL | brown sugar (lightly packed) | 1 c. |
| 250 mL | white sugar | 1 c. |
| 2 | eggs | 2 |
| 10 mL | vanilla | 2 tsp. |
| 375 mL | all-purpose flour | 1½ c. |
| 5 mL | baking soda | 1 tsp. |
| 2 mL | salt | ½ tsp. |
| 750 mL | quick-cooking (not instant) oatmeal | 3 c. |
| | candies for decoration | |

large mixing bowl, wooden spoon, wax paper, rolling pin, dinosaur cookie cutter, lifter, baking sheet lined with aluminum foil, cooling rack

1 Preheat the oven to 180°C (350°F).

2 Beat together the shortening and sugars until creamy. Stir in the eggs and vanilla. Add the flour, baking soda and salt. Blend well. Stir in the oatmeal.

3 Following the instructions on page 5, roll out some dough until it is 1 cm (⅜ in.) thick, or flatten it with clean hands. Cut out cookies using the cookie cutter. With the lifter, transfer cookies to the baking sheet, placing them about 5 cm (2 in.) apart. Repeat with remaining dough. Decorate with candies.

4 Bake 10 to 12 minutes, until golden. Cool for 3 minutes, then transfer cookies to the cooling rack. Cool completely.

*Makes about 5 dozen cookies*

## OTHER IDEAS

★ Add to the dough 250 mL (1 c.) chocolate chips, raisins, baking jujubes, chopped gumdrops, or coconut and dried pineapple bits.

★ Roll out or flatten the dough and cut it into rectangles. Decorate them to make greeting cards, gift tags or place cards.

★ Bake the dough as one large cookie in whatever shape you like — a friend's face, an apple for your teacher, a birthday cake — and "glue" candy decorations in place with melted chocolate (page 5).

## WRAP IT UP

★ Make a flat bag for your dinosaur. Cut a piece of wax paper slightly more than twice as big as the cookie.

Fold it in half and glue two edges together.

When the glue is dry, decorate the bag with stickers. Place your cookie in the bag and hold it closed with colorful paper clips or two decorated magnets.

# Quick chocolate balls

*Whip up some for Mother's Day — you won't need her help to make these no-bake treats.*

## YOU WILL NEED

| | | |
|---|---|---|
| 175 mL | white sugar | ¾ c. |
| 125 mL | butter (room temperature) | ½ c. |
| 25 mL | milk | 2 tbsp. |
| 10 mL | vanilla | 2 tsp. |
| 500 mL | quick-cooking (not instant) oatmeal | 2 c. |
| 50 mL | unsweetened cocoa powder | ¼ c. |
| 50 mL | chopped pecans | ¼ c. |
| 50 mL | sweetened flaked (or shredded) coconut | ¼ c. |
| large mixing bowl, wooden spoon, sifter, 2 small plates | | |

**1** Beat together the sugar and butter until creamy. Stir in the milk and vanilla. Add the oatmeal and sift cocoa over the mixture. Blend well.

**2** Form the dough into 2.5 cm (1 in.) balls.

**3** Pour the pecans and coconut onto separate plates. Roll half the balls in the pecans. Roll the other half in coconut.

Refrigerate for up to 1 week or freeze for up to 2 months.

*Makes about 2½ dozen balls*

## OTHER IDEAS

★ Make these cookies for Father's Day too. If Dad doesn't like pecans, replace them with his favorite nut.

★ Add 125 mL (½ c.) raisins, dried cranberries or your mom or dad's favorite dried fruit.

# Brownies

*A sweet treat for a faraway friend.*
*To mail, wrap them in plastic wrap*
*and pack in a sturdy box.*

## YOU WILL NEED

| | | |
|---|---|---|
| 175 mL | butter, melted (page 5) | ¾ c. |
| 4 | squares unsweetened chocolate, melted (page 5) | 4 |
| 375 mL | white sugar | 1½ c. |
| 3 | eggs | 3 |
| 5 mL | vanilla | 1 tsp. |
| 175 mL | all-purpose flour | ¾ c. |
| 1 mL | salt | ¼ tsp. |
| 175 mL | chopped walnuts | ¾ c. |
| 125 mL | chocolate chips | ½ c. |

small mixing bowl, wooden spoon,
large mixing bowl, 20 cm (8 in.) square
cake pan lined with aluminum foil,
cooling rack

**1** Preheat the oven to 180°C (350°F).

**2** In the small bowl, mix the butter and chocolate. Refrigerate 15 minutes, until at room temperature.

**3** In the large bowl, stir the sugar and eggs until pale yellow. Add the vanilla. Mix in the chocolate mixture until well combined. Gently stir in the flour and salt. Add the walnuts and chocolate chips. Stir well.

**4** Pour the batter into the pan. Bake 40 to 45 minutes, until sides have pulled away from the pan but the center is soft. Cool completely in the pan on the cooling rack.

*Makes about 2 dozen brownies*

## OTHER IDEAS

★ When the brownies are still warm, place 25 Hershey's Kisses on top in five rows of five.

★ Cut the brownies into squares, and dust half of each with icing sugar.

# Pinwheels

*Perfect for a windy spring day
— watch them zoom off the plate.*

## YOU WILL NEED

| | | |
|---|---|---|
| 250 mL | white sugar | 1 c. |
| 50 mL | butter (room temperature) | ¼ c. |
| 50 mL | shortening (room temperature) | ¼ c. |
| 1 | egg | 1 |
| 5 mL | vanilla | 1 tsp. |
| 500 mL | all-purpose flour | 2 c. |
| 5 mL | baking powder | 1 tsp. |
| 125 mL | colored sugar or sprinkles or chopped walnuts | ½ c. |

large mixing bowl, wooden spoon,
plastic wrap, wax paper, rolling pin,
table knife, lifter, baking sheet lined
with aluminum foil, cooling rack

**1** Beat together the white sugar, butter and shortening until creamy. Stir in the egg and vanilla. Add the flour and baking powder. Blend well. Wrap the dough in plastic and refrigerate 1 hour, until firm.

**2** Preheat the oven to 190°C (375°F).

**3** Following the instructions on page 5, roll out some dough until it is 0.3 cm (⅛ in.) thick. Cut the dough into 7.5 cm (3 in.) squares. With the lifter, transfer cookies to the baking sheet, placing them about 4 cm (1½ in.) apart. Sprinkle the cookies with colored sugar, sprinkles or walnuts. Repeat with remaining dough.

**4** Cut the squares from each corner almost to the center, as shown. Fold every other point to the center, and gently press together.

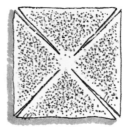 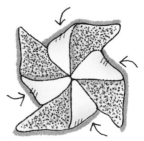

**5** Bake 6 to 8 minutes, until golden. Cool for 3 minutes, then transfer cookies to the cooling rack. Cool completely.

*Makes about 2 dozen cookies*

# Mud cookies

*Spring brings warm days, flowers, rainbows — and mud. Whoever thought it could taste so delicious?*

## YOU WILL NEED

| | | |
|---|---|---|
| 500 mL | chocolate chips | 2 c. |
| 50 mL | butter | ¼ c. |
| 1 | 300 mL (10 oz.) can sweetened condensed milk | 1 |
| 375 mL | all-purpose flour | 1½ c. |

medium saucepan, wooden spoon, baking sheet lined with aluminum foil, lifter, cooling rack

**1** Preheat the oven to 180°C (350°F).

**2** With an adult's help, place the chocolate chips and butter in the saucepan and melt over low heat, stirring constantly for 5 minutes, until smooth. Remove from heat.

**3** Add the sweetened condensed milk and flour. Stir until smooth.

**4** Form the dough into 2.5 cm (1 in.) balls. Place on the baking sheet about 4 cm (1½ in.) apart.

**5** Bake 6 to 8 minutes, until just firm. Cool for 3 minutes, then transfer cookies to the cooling rack. Cool completely.

*Makes about 4 dozen cookies*

### WRAP IT UP

★ Line a clean flowerpot with a piece of cellophane. Make a paper or felt flower and glue it to a pipe cleaner, clean twig or stick. Let dry. Stand the flower in the pot and fill with cookies. Gather the cellophane around the stem and tie with a bow.

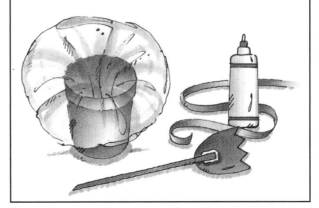

# Watermelons

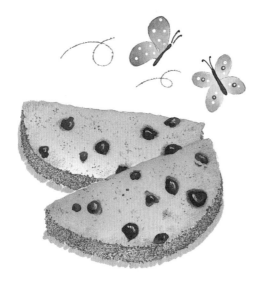

*You know it's summer when you can't wait to bite into a sweet slice of watermelon.*

## YOU WILL NEED

| | | |
|---|---|---|
| 175 mL | butter (room temperature) | ¾ c. |
| 125 mL | white sugar | ½ c. |
| 1 | 85 g (3 oz.) package watermelon gelatin powder | 1 |
| 1 | egg | 1 |
| | red food coloring | |
| 425 mL | all-purpose flour | 1¾ c. |
| 2 mL | baking powder | ½ tsp. |
| 75 mL | miniature chocolate chips | ⅓ c. |
| 45 mL | green sugar | 3 tbsp. |

large mixing bowl, wooden spoon, wax paper, large plate, kitchen knife, baking sheet lined with aluminum foil, lifter, cooling rack

1 Cream together the butter, white sugar and gelatin powder until fluffy. Add the egg and beat until smooth. Mix in about 8 drops of food coloring. Stir in the flour and baking powder. Blend well. Stir in the chocolate chips.

2 Divide the dough in half and shape each half into a log 12.5 cm (5 in.) long. Wrap in wax paper and refrigerate for 2 hours.

3 Preheat the oven to 180°C (350°F).

4 Pour the green sugar onto the plate, and roll each log in it. Cut the dough into slices 0.5 cm (¼ in.) thick, then cut each slice in half. Place on the baking sheet about 4 cm (1½ in.) apart.

5 Bake 8 to 10 minutes, until just firm. Cool for 3 minutes, then transfer cookies to the cooling rack. Cool completely.

*Makes about 8 dozen cookies*

# Coconutty chews

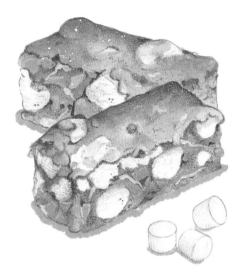

*Chill out with no-bake bars.*

## YOU WILL NEED

| | | |
|---|---|---|
| 250 mL | white sugar | 1 c. |
| 2 | eggs (beaten) | 2 |
| 175 mL | butter | ¾ c. |
| 10 mL | vanilla | 2 tsp. |
| 625 mL | miniature marshmallows | 2½ c. |
| 300 mL | graham wafer crumbs | 1¼ c. |
| 250 mL | sweetened flaked (or shredded) coconut | 1 c. |
| 250 mL | chopped walnuts | 1 c. |

medium saucepan, wooden spoon, 20 cm (8 in.) square cake pan lined with aluminum foil

**1** In the saucepan, combine the sugar and eggs. Add the butter. With an adult's help, warm the mixture over medium heat, stirring constantly for about 5 minutes, until thickened. Stir in the vanilla.

**2** Refrigerate for about 30 minutes, stirring occasionally, until at room temperature.

**3** Add the marshmallows, graham crumbs, coconut and walnuts. Stir well.

**4** Press the mixture into the pan and refrigerate about 20 minutes, until firm.

Refrigerate for up to 2 weeks.

*Makes about 2½ dozen bars*

## OTHER IDEAS

★ Drizzle melted chocolate (page 5) over the finished bars.

★ Replace the graham wafer crumbs with chocolate wafer crumbs, or the coconut with chocolate chips.

# Peanut butter cookies

*Welcome autumn with great
fall-colored cookies.*

## YOU WILL NEED

| | | |
|---|---|---|
| 250 mL | smooth or crunchy peanut butter (a commercial brand, not natural) | 1 c. |
| 175 mL | white sugar | ¾ c. |
| 1 | egg | 1 |
| 125 mL | Reese's Pieces | ½ c. |

large mixing bowl, wooden spoon,
baking sheet lined with aluminum foil,
fork, lifter, cooling rack

**1** Preheat the oven to 180°C (350°F).

**2** Cream together the peanut butter and sugar until well blended. Mix in the egg, then stir in the Reese's Pieces.

**3** Form the dough into 2.5 cm (1 in.) balls. Place on the baking sheet about 4 cm (1½ in.) apart and flatten with the fork.

**4** Bake 8 to 10 minutes, until firm. Cool for 5 minutes, then transfer cookies to the cooling rack. Cool completely.

*Makes about 2½ dozen cookies*

## WRAP IT UP

★ Decorate a paper bag, then place plastic-wrapped cookies inside. Fold the bag closed, and cut six slits. Lace a ribbon through the slits, and tie in a bow.

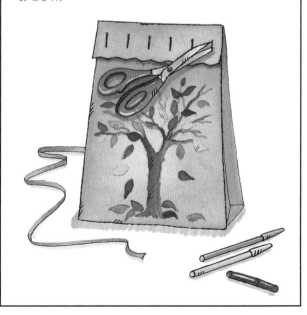

# Butterscotch almond bars

*Nothing says autumn like a batch of buttery, nutty squares.*

## YOU WILL NEED

| | | |
|---|---|---|
| 250 mL | all-purpose flour | 1 c. |
| 250 mL | quick-cooking (not instant) oatmeal | 1 c. |
| 250 mL | brown sugar (lightly packed) | 1 c. |
| 5 mL | baking soda | 1 tsp. |
| 125 mL | butter (room temperature) | ½ c. |
| 125 mL | corn syrup | ½ c. |
| 75 mL | brown sugar (lightly packed) | ⅓ c. |
| 50 mL | butter | ¼ c. |
| 50 mL | milk | ¼ c. |
| 10 mL | vanilla | 2 tsp. |
| 375 mL | sliced almonds | 1½ c. |

large mixing bowl, wooden spoon, 23 cm x 33 cm (9 in. x 13 in.) cake pan lined with aluminum foil, fork, medium saucepan, cooling rack, table knife

1 Preheat the oven to 180°C (350°F).

2 Combine the flour, oatmeal, 250 mL (1 c.) brown sugar and baking soda. Add 125 mL (½ c.) butter and mix until crumbly. Press the mixture firmly into the pan. Bake 10 to 12 minutes, until golden.

3 In the saucepan, stir together the corn syrup, brown sugar, butter and milk. With an adult's help, cook over medium heat just until the mixture boils, then remove from heat. Stir in the vanilla, then the almonds. Pour over the crust, making sure the almonds are spread evenly.

4 Bake 15 to 18 minutes, until golden. Partially cool in the pan on the cooling rack. While still warm, cut into bars or triangles.

Refrigerate for up to 1 week or freeze for up to 2 months.

*Makes about 3 dozen bars*

# Chocolate chip cookies

*On a cold winter day, what could taste better than a mug of hot chocolate and these classic cookies?*

## YOU WILL NEED

| | | |
|---|---|---|
| 250 mL | butter (room temperature) | 1 c. |
| 175 mL | white sugar | ¾ c. |
| 175 mL | brown sugar (lightly packed) | ¾ c. |
| 2 | eggs | 2 |
| 10 mL | vanilla | 2 tsp. |
| 550 mL | all-purpose flour | 2¼ c. |
| 5 mL | baking soda | 1 tsp. |
| 2 mL | salt | ½ tsp. |
| 375 mL | chocolate chips | 1½ c. |

large mixing bowl, wooden spoon, teaspoon, baking sheet lined with aluminum foil, lifter, cooling rack

**1** Preheat the oven to 180°C (350°F).

**2** Beat together the butter and sugars until creamy. Stir in the eggs and vanilla. Add the flour, baking soda and salt. Blend well. Stir in the chocolate chips.

**3** Drop the dough by teaspoonful onto the baking sheet about 4 cm (1½ in.) apart.

**4** Bake 8 to 10 minutes, until golden. Cool for 3 minutes, then transfer cookies to the cooling rack. Cool completely.

*Makes about 5 dozen cookies*

## OTHER IDEAS

★ Make Dirt Cookies by replacing the chocolate chips with crumbled chocolate sandwich cookies (about 20 cookies).

★ Dip cooled cookies into melted white or dark chocolate (page 5) so they are half covered.

# Shining stars

*As beautiful as twinkling stars on a crisp winter night, but much tastier!*

## YOU WILL NEED

| | | |
|---|---|---|
| 250 mL | butter (room temperature) | 1 c. |
| 250 mL | icing sugar | 1 c. |
| 1 | egg | 1 |
| 10 mL | vanilla | 2 tsp. |
| 625 mL | all-purpose flour | 2½ c. |
| 2 mL | baking soda | ½ tsp. |
| 1 mL | salt | ¼ tsp. |
| 125 mL | jam or jelly | ½ c. |

large mixing bowl, wooden spoon, wax paper, rolling pin, a medium and a small star-shaped cookie cutter, lifter, baking sheet lined with aluminum foil, cooling rack, table knife

**1** Preheat the oven to 180°C (350°F).

**2** Beat together the butter and icing sugar until fluffy. Stir in the egg and vanilla. Add the flour, baking soda and salt. Blend well.

**3** Following the instructions on page 5, roll out some dough until it is 0.3 cm (⅛ in.) thick. Cut out cookies with the medium cookie cutter. Cut stars in the center of half the cookies using the small cutter. With the lifter, transfer cookies to the baking sheet, placing them about 4 cm (1½ in.) apart. Repeat with remaining dough.

**4** Bake 10 to 12 minutes, until golden. Cool for 3 minutes, then transfer cookies to the cooling rack. Cool completely.

**5** Spread jam on the whole cookies and top them with the cookies with cutouts, top side up.

Store at room temperature for up to 1 week or freeze, without jam, for up to 2 months.

*Makes about 2 dozen cookies*

# Potato chippers

*If you feel like having a cookie that's sweet and salty, try this combo.*

## YOU WILL NEED

| | | |
|---|---|---|
| 250 mL | white sugar | 1 c. |
| 125 mL | butter (room temperature) | ½ c. |
| 125 mL | shortening (room temperature) | ½ c. |
| 2 | eggs | 2 |
| 10 mL | vanilla | 2 tsp. |
| 625 mL | all-purpose flour | 2½ c. |
| 2 mL | salt | ½ tsp. |
| 375 mL | crushed barbeque potato chips | 1½ c. |
| 125 mL | chopped pecans | ½ c. |

large mixing bowl, wooden spoon, teaspoon, baking sheet lined with aluminum foil, lifter, cooling rack

**1** Preheat the oven to 180°C (350°F).

**2** Beat together the sugar, butter and shortening until creamy. Stir in the eggs and vanilla. Add the flour and salt. Blend well. Mix in the chips and pecans.

**3** Drop the dough by teaspoonful onto the baking sheet about 4 cm (1½ in.) apart.

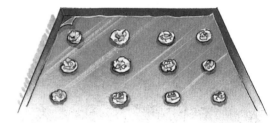

**4** Bake 10 to 12 minutes, until light golden. Cool for 3 minutes, then transfer cookies to the cooling rack. Cool completely.

*Makes about 4 dozen cookies*

## OTHER IDEAS

★ Use a different flavor of potato chip.

★ Add 125 mL (½ c.) chocolate chips to the dough, or drizzle melted chocolate (page 5) on cooled cookies.

# Crazy daisies

*Give your teacher a bouquet of these wacky daisies.*

## YOU WILL NEED

| | | |
|---|---|---|
| 250 mL | white sugar | 1 c. |
| 175 mL | butter (room temperature) | ¾ c. |
| 1 | egg | 1 |
| 10 mL | vanilla | 2 tsp. |
| 550 mL | all-purpose flour | 2¼ c. |
| | colored sugars | |

large mixing bowl, wooden spoon, small plate, baking sheet lined with aluminum foil, kitchen knife, lifter, cooling rack

**1** Preheat the oven to 190°C (375°F).

**2** Beat together the white sugar and butter until creamy. Stir in the egg and vanilla. Blend in the flour.

**3** Form dough into 3 cm (1¼ in.) balls. Pour some colored sugar onto the plate, and roll the balls in it. Place on the baking sheet about 4 cm (1½ in.) apart.

**4** In each ball, make three cuts a little more than halfway down, as shown. Spread the sections slightly to form petals. Sprinkle different colored sugar in each cookie's center.

**5** Bake 10 to 12 minutes, until golden. Cool for 3 minutes, then transfer cookies to the cooling rack. Cool completely.

*Makes about 3 dozen cookies*

## WRAP IT UP

★ Decoupage a box. Mix equal amounts of white glue and water. Dip small pieces of wrapping paper in the mixture, and smooth them onto the box. When dry, cover with two coats of acrylic varnish. Let dry after each coat.

# Magic cookie wands

*Make someone's wish for great
cookies come true.*

## YOU WILL NEED

| | | |
|---|---|---|
| 250 mL | white sugar | 1 c. |
| 125 mL | shortening (room temperature) | ½ c. |
| 1 | egg | 1 |
| 25 mL | milk | 2 tbsp. |
| 5 mL | vanilla | 1 tsp. |
| 425 mL | all-purpose flour | 1¾ c. |
| 5 mL | baking powder | 1 tsp. |
| 2 mL | baking soda | ½ tsp. |
| 2 mL | salt | ½ tsp. |
| 10 | small mint patties (cut in half) | 10 |

large mixing bowl, wooden spoon, wax
paper, rolling pin, medium star-shaped
cookie cutter, lifter, baking sheet lined with
aluminum foil, 20 long sticks, cooling rack

1 Preheat the oven to 190°C (375°F).

2 Beat together the sugar and shortening until fluffy. Stir in the egg, milk and vanilla. Add the flour, baking powder, baking soda and salt. Blend well.

3 Following the instructions on page 5, roll out half the dough until it is 0.3 cm (⅛ in.) thick. Cut out cookies with the cookie cutter. With the lifter, transfer cookies to the baking sheet, placing them about 5 cm (2 in.) apart. Place a stick and a mint patty half on each star as shown.

4 Roll out the remaining dough and cut out stars. Use the lifter to place them on the other cookies. Press gently around the edges.

5 Bake 8 to 10 minutes, until golden. Cool for 3 minutes, then transfer cookies to the cooling rack. Cool completely.

*Makes about 20 cookies*

# Slowpokes

*These cookies look like slow, pokey turtles.*
*Perfect for a friend who's always late.*

## YOU WILL NEED

| | | |
|---|---|---|
| 2 | squares unsweetened chocolate | 2 |
| 75 mL | shortening | ⅓ c. |
| 2 | eggs | 2 |
| 250 mL | white sugar | 1 c. |
| 175 mL | all-purpose flour | ¾ c. |
| 2 mL | baking powder | ½ tsp. |
| 1 mL | salt | ¼ tsp. |
| 250 mL | pecan halves | 1 c. |
| 500 mL | icing sugar | 2 c. |
| 125 mL | unsweetened cocoa powder (sifted) | ½ c. |
| 50 mL | butter (room temperature) | ¼ c. |
| 45 mL | milk | 3 tbsp. |

large microwavable bowl, wooden spoon, baking sheet lined with aluminum foil, teaspoon, lifter, cooling rack, medium mixing bowl, table knife

1 Preheat the oven to 190°C (375°F).

2 Place the chocolate and shortening in the large bowl. With an adult's help, microwave about 1½ minutes, until just melted, stirring every 30 seconds. Stir in the eggs and white sugar. Add the flour, baking powder and salt. Blend well.

3 For each cookie, place three pecan halves on the baking sheet as shown, about 4 cm (1½ in.) apart. Drop a small teaspoon of dough onto the middle of the nuts.

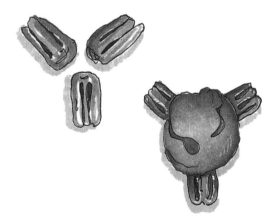

4 Bake 10 to 12 minutes, until firm. Cool for 3 minutes, then transfer cookies to the cooling rack. Cool completely.

5 For the icing, beat together the remaining ingredients in the medium bowl until creamy. Swirl icing over each cookie.

*Makes about 3 dozen cookies*

# Pretzels

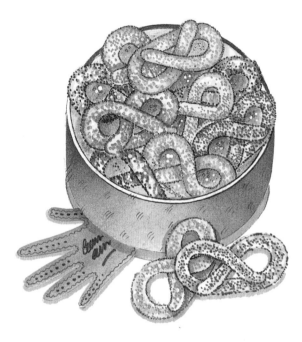

*Surprise a pretzel lover with a bowl of sweet, twisty treats.*

## YOU WILL NEED

| | | |
|---|---|---|
| 125 mL | butter (room temperature) | ½ c. |
| 50 mL | white sugar | ¼ c. |
| 1 | egg | 1 |
| 5 mL | vanilla | 1 tsp. |
| 375 mL | all-purpose flour | 1½ c. |
| | colored sugars | |

large mixing bowl, wooden spoon, teaspoon, wax paper, lifter, baking sheet lined with aluminum foil, cooling rack

**1** Preheat the oven to 190°C (375°F).

**2** Beat together the butter and white sugar until creamy. Stir in the egg and vanilla. Blend in the flour.

**3** For each cookie, place a teaspoonful of dough on lightly floured wax paper. With your palm, roll the dough into a rope 25 cm (10 in.) long and as thick as a pencil. Twist it into a pretzel, as shown. With the lifter, carefully transfer pretzels to the baking sheet, placing them about 2.5 cm (1 in.) apart. Sprinkle with colored sugar.

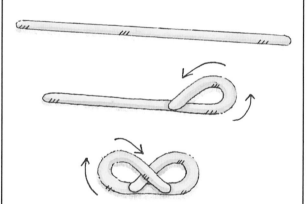

**4** Bake 10 to 12 minutes, until golden. Cool for 3 minutes, then transfer cookies to the cooling rack. Cool completely.

*Makes about 2½ dozen pretzels*

## WRAP IT UP

★ Make a gift card. Trace around your hand on thick paper and cut it out. Add the receiver's name, and decorate.

# Chocolate sandwiches

*These cookies will brighten anyone's day.*

## YOU WILL NEED

| | | |
|---|---|---|
| 250 mL | white sugar | 1 c. |
| 125 mL | butter (room temperature) | ½ c. |
| 125 mL | shortening (room temperature) | ½ c. |
| 1 | egg | 1 |
| 25 mL | milk | 2 tbsp. |
| 500 mL | all-purpose flour | 2 c. |
| 125 mL | unsweetened cocoa powder | ½ c. |
| 2 mL | baking soda | ½ tsp. |
| 500 mL | icing sugar | 2 c. |
| 50 mL | butter (room temperature) | ¼ c. |
| 45 mL | milk | 3 tbsp. |
| 2 mL | vanilla | ½ tsp. |
| | food coloring | |

large mixing bowl, wooden spoon, sifter, wax paper, rolling pin, round cookie cutter or glass, lifter, baking sheet lined with aluminum foil, cooling rack, medium mixing bowl, table knife

1 Preheat the oven to 190°C (375°F).

2 In the large bowl, beat together the white sugar, 125 mL (½ c.) butter and shortening until creamy. Stir in the egg and 25 mL (2 tbsp.) milk. Sift the flour, cocoa and baking soda over the mixture. Blend well.

3 Following the instructions on page 5, roll out some dough until it is 0.3 cm (⅛ in.) thick. Cut out cookies using the cookie cutter or glass. With the lifter, transfer cookies to the baking sheet, placing them about 4 cm (1½ in.) apart. Repeat with remaining dough.

4 Bake 6 to 8 minutes, until the edges are firm. Cool for 3 minutes, then transfer cookies to the cooling rack. Cool completely.

5 For the icing, beat the icing sugar, butter, milk and vanilla in the medium bowl until creamy. Add as much food coloring as you like. Mix well.

6 For each sandwich, spread icing on the bottom of a cookie. Place another cookie on top, top side up.

*Makes about 2 dozen sandwiches*

# Thumbprints

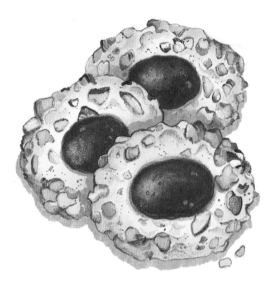

*Bake these cookies for your next DVD party — your friends will definitely give them two thumbs up!*

## YOU WILL NEED

| | | |
|---|---|---|
| 250 mL | butter (room temperature) | 1 c. |
| 125 mL | brown sugar (lightly packed) | ½ c. |
| 1 | egg | 1 |
| 10 mL | vanilla | 2 tsp. |
| 500 mL | all-purpose flour | 2 c. |
| 1 mL | salt | ¼ tsp. |
| 175 mL | finely chopped walnuts | ¾ c. |
| 150 mL | jam or jelly | ⅔ c. |

large mixing bowl, wooden spoon, small plate, baking sheet lined with aluminum foil, lifter, cooling rack, teaspoon

1 Preheat the oven to 180°C (350°F).

2 Beat together the butter and sugar until creamy. Stir in the egg and vanilla. Add the flour and salt. Mix well.

3 Form the dough into 2.5 cm (1 in.) balls. Place the walnuts on the plate, and roll the balls in them. Place on the baking sheet about 2.5 cm (1 in.) apart. With your thumb, make an indent in each cookie.

4 Bake 10 minutes, until firm. Cool for 3 minutes, then transfer cookies to the cooling rack. Cool completely.

5 Fill each indent with jam.

*Makes about 3½ dozen cookies*

## OTHER IDEAS

★ When cookies are just out of the oven, fill each indent with a Hershey's Kiss or chocolate chips, instead of jam.

# Snickerdoodles

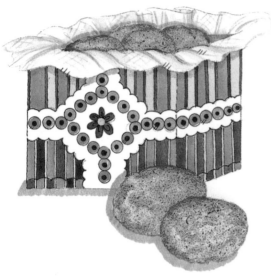

*The goofy name will make your family laugh, and the spicy flavor will keep them smiling.*

## YOU WILL NEED

| | | |
|---|---|---|
| 175 mL | white sugar | ¾ c. |
| 125 mL | butter (room temperature) | ½ c. |
| 1 | egg | 1 |
| 10 mL | vanilla | 2 tsp. |
| 325 mL | all-purpose flour | 1⅓ c. |
| 10 mL | baking powder | 2 tsp. |
| 1 mL | salt | ¼ tsp. |
| 15 mL | white sugar | 1 tbsp. |
| 5 mL | cinnamon | 1 tsp. |

large mixing bowl, wooden spoon, small plate, baking sheet lined with aluminum foil, lifter, cooling rack

**1** Preheat the oven to 190°C (375°F).

**2** Beat together 175 mL (¾ c.) sugar and the butter until fluffy. Stir in the egg and vanilla. Add the flour, baking powder and salt. Blend well.

**3** On the plate, stir together the sugar and cinnamon. Form the dough into 2.5 cm (1 in.) balls, and roll them in the sugar mixture. Place cookies on the baking sheet about 4 cm (1½ in.) apart.

**4** Bake 12 to 15 minutes, until the edges are golden. Cool for 3 minutes, then transfer cookies to the cooling rack. Cool completely.

*Makes about 2 dozen cookies*

## WRAP IT UP

★ Wrap or paint a box, then glue on buttons to make a funky pattern, caterpillar or flowers. Decorate with ribbons or markers. You can also make a card with buttons.

# Honeybees

*Here's a wacky way to ask someone to "bee" your "honey"!*

## YOU WILL NEED

| | | |
|---|---|---|
| 50 mL | smooth peanut butter (a commercial brand, not natural) | ¼ c. |
| 50 mL | shortening (room temperature) | ¼ c. |
| 50 mL | brown sugar (lightly packed) | ¼ c. |
| 1 | egg | 1 |
| 50 mL | liquid honey | ¼ c. |
| 5 mL | vanilla | 1 tsp. |
| 250 mL | all-purpose flour | 1 c. |
| 2 mL | baking soda | ½ tsp. |
| 60 | mini pretzel twists | 60 |
| 50 mL | chocolate chips | ¼ c. |

large mixing bowl, wooden spoon, baking sheet lined with aluminum foil, teaspoon, lifter, cooling rack

**1** Preheat the oven to 180°C (350°F).

**2** Beat together the peanut butter, shortening and sugar until well mixed. Stir in the egg, honey and vanilla. Add the flour and baking soda. Blend well.

**3** For each cookie, place two pretzels on the baking sheet with the bottoms touching, as shown, about 4 cm (1½ in.) apart. Form a teaspoonful of dough into a 4 cm (1½ in.) long log, place it where the pretzels touch and flatten slightly.

**4** Bake 10 to 12 minutes, until golden. Cool for 3 minutes, then transfer cookies to the cooling rack. Cool completely.

**5** With an adult's help, melt the chocolate chips (page 5). Drizzle the melted chocolate on the bees' "bodies" to look like stripes.

*Makes about 2½ dozen cookies*

## OTHER IDEAS

★ Add 125 mL (½ c.) chocolate or peanut butter chips.